BIRDHOUSES MADE OF BULLET HOLES

POEMS ON RETURN

Noeme Grace C. Tabor-Farjani

FOLKWAYS PRESS, LLC

Texas, USA
www.folkwayspress.com

Birdhouses Made of Bullet Holes
first published in 2025

Text © Noeme Grace C. Tabor-Farjani, 2025

Cover design by Julie Raven

ISBN: 978-1-7362701-5-8.

All rights reserved. This publication may not be reproduced, stored in a retrieval system or transmitted, in any form or by any means – electronic, mechanical, photocopying, recording or otherwise, without the prior permission of the publisher

CONTENTS

About the Author	VII
Birdhouses Made of Bullet Holes	1
The Clouds of August	5
Day 79	7
A Toast to Arriving	9
Where No One Knows	11
Mercy	12
The Way Back	14
On Pain, or Ruminations on a Broken Foot	16
The Way to Die	18
Cleaning Up	20
The Chaos of Open Skies	22
Episode	24
Advise to Self	26
Watching Caged Birds	27
July in Review	28
Emotional Landfill	30
Reprise from Song of Stars	31
Why I Write	34
The Inbox Becomes a Confessional	36
Whirlwind In My Mind	38

Self-regulation	40
Ars Poetica with Dialogues	41
For Alton	43
Not a Season of Writing	45
Escape Artist	46
Therapy Session	48
Survival Tactic	50
Leaving	51
For Now There Is Only (IV)	53
Panic Attack	55
Dissipated Rage on Valentine's Day	57
My Son Tells Me	59
Tea Time	60
Adrift	62
Self-Soothing	63
Seeing Shadows	65
From Meditation	66
June in Review	67
Tails of the last year, in words	69
I know this feeling, but	71
An Honest Exchange	74
Writing in Autumn	76
Recovery	78
Check Up	80
Racing Thoughts	82

from The Journal of Existential Dread	83
In My Living Room	85
Visions	88
Birdhouses in Bullet Holes	89
After the Sandstorm	91
Settlement	92
In My House Back Home	93
swim then fly away	95
Reflections on Poems and on Return	96

ABOUT THE AUTHOR

Noeme Grace C Tabor-Farjani, PhD, is a Tripoli, Libya-based Filipino poet, educator, and memoirist. She is the author of the poetry collections *The Gospel of Grace* (UK: Newcomer Press, 2021) which American writer Sonya Huber blurbed as a blending of Adrienne Rich and Tillie Olsen, and *Inspecting Wastelands* (Canada: Ukiyoto Publishing, 2023) as well as the prose chapbook, *Letters from Libya: Letters-in-Memoirs* (2018), which chronicles her family's escape from the Second Libyan Civil War. She has been published in journals and magazines such as *433 Magazine, Harpy Hybrid Review*, and *Rogue Agent Journal* (United States), *Voice & Verse Poetry Magazine* (Hong Kong), *Olongo Africa* (Nigeria), *Rusted Radishes* (Lebanon), *Eunoia Review* (Singapore), *The Bosphorus Review of Books* (Turkey), *Rowayat Journal* (Egypt), *Prairie Fire Magazine* (Canada), and elsewhere in New Zealand, Ireland, Australia, and India. She has also contributed to British and American anthologies such as *Hair Raising* (Nine Pens Press), *Things That Go Bump in the Night* (Dreich Press), *Plant People: An Anthology of Environmental Artists* (Plants & Poetry), and *Neurodiverse: Poetry by Neurodivergent Writers* (Flapjack Press). A featured author at the Heartland Society of Women Writers in Indiana and GMA Regional TV in the Philippines, she was a recipient of Para Site-Hong Kong's NoExit Grant for Unpaid Artistic Labour in 2021. She is currently working on her first full-length memoir. More of her works at https://linktr.ee/noemegracetf.

… BIRDHOUSES MADE OF
BULLET HOLES

For T. & the Fourjanis SKHZ

THE CLOUDS OF AUGUST

Flimsy and light cirrus forming
seahorse, angel wings,
horseshoe, swans, and hearts
splitting into lovers gazing
at each other's faces
each half of a twin.

Summer makes the best
of its showdown on blue skies,
like a broadcast of a TV special.

I watch them: cotton, marble
with purple and yellow streaks,
turning my awe into a mixture
of smiles and sniffles.

This parade of sentimentality
reminds me how to disappear
with style, by leaving traces
and coming back, unrecognized.

Such sacredness, divine techniques
of guilt-free tripping over earth
impossible to capture
and replicate.

DAY 79

I try to afford the delusions of being
    at home with myself
settling like a scavenger of fantasies packed
    in forgotten luggage.

The early bird catches the crescent spring moon
    on this last quarter
of our first one hundred days after migration.

Time inches, a seducer languid in my bed
    while I cast myself into
the mercies of the moon cycle and dispose
    my stashing of regrets.

I await my fill of days in this branded golden
    cage, complete with amenities
and a luxury of whims lined up as to-do list
    since I have nowhere to go.

I am obedient to rules, regulating my affairs
    around calls for prayers, contented

with a thousand consolation prizes made
    of well-enunciated *InshaAllah*.

The rectangular walls are whiteboards of hope,
    my sole preoccupation other than
the guessing games I play with the hours while I
    figure my way around here.

It's hard to tell right from wrong as I trace
    the Moorish curves of the window railing,
like the maze of lies that coil around reason
    tinted with excuses.

This little creature perched on the sill must be
    comparing my space with the sky,
perhaps planning where to fly next or deciding
    to stay a bit longer.

It pecks the tiny crack on the wall, crumbs
    of bread lay on the bullet hole. A feeder
by chance that was once a hazard to the robin's
    ancestors who eat and worry later.

They seem to have no need for fantasies,
    but who knows. *InshaAllah*, soon, maybe.

A TOAST TO ARRIVING

Here's to all the baggage we've trundled
along this move to return.
We're still half-aliens, but we arrived,
unscathed by bureaucracy,
as the oath to make them pay dissolves
like ink on wet paper.
Like how our names, phone numbers,
email, and country name turn into shadows,
smudges on plastic luggage tags.
But at least we got them all, each for the six
of us: four beaten, old hand-me-downs
from family back home, and two new ones,
the cheapest we could find.
I swear to not use marker on these tags again,
you swear to never go back to my country.
Here's to everything we've packed
to take with us—gifts from home, seedlings,
and the hope to grow them here,
gifts for home, the boys' guitars and gadgets
and sentimentality in clothes
we cannot wear in this season.

NOEME GRACE C. TABOR-FARJANI

Here's to arriving after the 20-hour journey
that sent you out like an infidel
to being welcomed like a hero.
The cheap transits in search of refuge,
and finding settlement on dirty airport floors
is a memory dissolved by tight,
warm embraces and happy tears.

WHERE NO ONE KNOWS

here is the certainty of desire,
and of its source despite a
numbness to this confinement

the view from here is clear as day,
bright outside the window, I could tell
knob from keyhole even with eyes closed

I feel hope rushing through closed doors,
barging in, insistent, imposing
like a storm indoors, gaining momentum

I see spirals of reason and faith,
bread and wine, rounding the rooms
here are words dripping off the floor
soon after they hit the ceiling, I clean up

soon, soon, the walls will go crashing down

MERCY

Bury that tag-along,
clothed like a seasoned traveler
but stuffed in your suitcase.
The dead could not easily sneak in a
baggage of countries
without being handed the keys.
Lay down to rest the memories,
down the womb of mercy
a doorway graced with spillage
from obligatory lovemaking
leading towards space,
black, hollow, galaxy of deaths
unworthy of beds, or floors,
or even walls around your head.
Bury all that's been said
that once caressed stab wounds
of its own making,
unworthy of lamentations.
Blood turns to blue, then black
to gray silvery stitches

MERCY

in sepultures that do not ache
with every touch.
End the tailgating of the dead,
and bury it deep, down
the womb of mercy
a portal of leaving, behind
a door where no ghost can re-enter.

THE WAY BACK

The pathways have changed
but failed to conceal
the traces of erasures
given the invention
of new plans to pay off debts,
rarely to return favors.
It is law to move forward.
A game in a progression
of jobs and bargaining
for salary increase,
the offers and rejections
are mixed with crumbs
scattered just in case
our memory fails
and we forget the map
of mistakes in our head.
Each step would maim us
from remembering
the leftover morsels

THE WAY BACK

in our pockets, but
I am pretty good at
resentments, that I
memorized the way back.

ON PAIN,

OR RUMINATIONS ON A BROKEN FOOT

This is symbolic, showing what I have
temporarily lost as one foot could not
carry on well without the other.
Black and white, working together
like these borrowed crutches,
like *up and down, close and open,
wet and dry, night and day, here and there,
you and me…*

Stillness puts them close to each other,
the big toes like beaks of lovebirds, kissing.
But one misstep, one failed to warn
Watch out or to watch the other out,
breaks a wing, or beak, or bone
followed by a fracture of everything else,
like plans and hearts, waiting to kiss again.

ON PAIN

Strangely, the other foot without the cast
begins to feel a burning sensation,
as if it is also injured.

Google says ...*the cells at the fracture site
release healing chemicals and signals
that cause new nerves to sprout.*
What sympathy, the ever-gracious
company of pain in an achingly dull
wrapping of time.

THE WAY TO DIE

What are the chances of a fish dying in an aquarium resembling an ocean?

Its life span should be longer in an imitated sea water, like air in cages for birds.

Still, they die earlier than those in habitat, earlier than caged birds.

Fish float dead on dirty aquarium water. Dead too, without water.

The same chances as this cleaner, malfunctioning. Congested with dust.

I remember to put everything in place and make a place for everything.

I forgot that is how things keep working, and people alive.

THE WAY TO DIE

I water the plants, wash the plates on time, clean the cat litter, cuddle the babies.

Stray from illness, and endure the prolonged pain, the perishing of passions.

Become a caricature of the screen, starving for faces I could touch, thirsty for home.

It's hard to tell between breath if my home is taken from me or I am removed from it.

I cannot tell an intruder from an abductor, invasion from expulsion.

But this cold, dry, closed, dark and lonely room shows me everything.

That this is not the way to live.

This is not even the way to die.

CLEANING UP

This place is smeared with longing
pressed against the glass window.
My hand traces the carvings of a locked door
as memory guides it down the knob
only to let the dead come
crashing in, and leave their litter
like a trail of the dumpster and the dumped
returning in order to proceed,
from the window to the door and vice versa.

One hand perpetually waits to be handed
the keys to the outside world,
while the other summons daily courage
to keep reaching down to gather
morsels of future-faking on the floor
and Freudian slips that fell of a mouth,
carefully hiding a fear of landmines
in a third-floor apartment.
I constantly wonder if there is indeed
clean sand like they say.

CLEANING UP

As if there's no need for dusting,
as if their sand is too proud to mingle
with my wrinkly hands that shift roles
between cleaner and cleaned,
making sure there's not a single trace
of desire left.

THE CHAOS OF OPEN SKIES

Three arms are outstretched unto the heavens,
like routes of consolation for the weary,
and mercy for the wretched.
Wonder is dead in the eyes of those
that caught the trickery of words,
and in the ears that once fell for songs,
a counterpoint of promises and secrets.
Yet some are still found grateful
for rigorous, entertaining show
and feign their amazement
at grand, magical gestures
of the generosity of sunbeams, not the sun.
They applaud the illusions
until the sky turns over
spilling misery, offering
a miracle water no one wants to buy,
or even take for free.

THE CHAOS OF OPEN SKIES

They know better how spells
are burned on paper,
mesmerizing like sunrise and sunset
and the ashes turn into white dove
soaring above an audience
that wants no peace nor purity
but chaos of the open skies.

EPISODE

You cannot,
even if you want to,
even if you try to,
feel the hundred sharp straws
stuck to my flesh, siphoning
my strength in regular intervals
of chilly days and hot flushes.

Even the happy hours
of blood and cells, courtesy
of short-lived shots of hope
you hand to me, cannot fix this.

I down your touch in one gasp
of air, the back rub
may be a reasonable thing to do
but it twists my stomach tighter
they could snap
into a series of blame-games

EPISODE

and accusations.
The paranoia,

I wonder why you cannot even
name a reason for keeping
me alive.

ADVISE TO SELF

Hide. Hide from prying eyes who mock the dreams they are feeding on; from those who herald double lives, hide your treasures but let its light

Shine. But inside closets, and shower, the chest boxes, blank pages, cereal bowls and tear-stained pillows. Shine them indoors, in feasts and confessionals, ash trays and hard-pressed cigarette stubs and cold coffee cups that heard secret conversations and witnessed endless stalking of the spotlight. Reveal your debt of light until you can

Soar. Way above the charm and mercies of thieves, beyond words written on fog, and characters on clouds. Soar through the applause, guiding your wings while your tail lights burn applauding hands. Drop it down to your aged rails of fool's gold. Drop them keys, let them. Let them cage that fire.

WATCHING CAGED BIRDS

Perhaps some birds are better off caged
in comfort behind railings of a home
free birds seek.
Maybe they are too splendid
for a sky that's full of song.
What service can they offer but captivity?
Perhaps some birds would rather stay in,
safe from an assault of doubts
that are carried by wind,
a perpetual courier of needs and wants.
What else is to be done with feeding trays
that are filled up to the brim, laid
before their full stomach?
Perhaps they are but accessories
to carry on a special mission
of relief for some early worms.

JULY IN REVIEW

On this 141st day of the many months
of disguising the chaos in my head
like a serene, well-poised diva
I am finally granted
a necessary shockwave,
distraction to a distraction.
I have no care for directions, shake me,
stir me up, push me away
anywhere, so long as it takes me away
from these doors swinging open
and close, as if moved by ghosts.
Take me away from the thumping
in my chest,
away from the traffic of rumors
in my head,
and scripted small talks,
the coming and going
of anticipation and suspicions.
I cringe at glimmers, a futility
that finds me loose yet lashing

JULY IN REVIEW

at this longing, resisting.
If I could just slap myself
from gawking at the ceiling
where I imagine your face,
or bang my head or better yet,
fireworks blasting near my ears
just to turn them deaf
to desire.
But this train keeps dragging me away,
far, far away, from these
doors *front, closets, cupboards,*
      to the backyard, bathroom, cabinets, eyes.
Everything I open leads to you.
There used to be only one door for home.

EMOTIONAL LANDFILL

what calcifies the heart?
resentment is like a plaque
made of what used to be
a luscious, rich, decadent
indulgence of a memory

REPRISE FROM SONG OF STARS

Scent of wood and musk, dried
 florals and breath,
soft, warm lights, crystals and
 tinkles of glasses,
echoes of animated conversations
 fill neighboring seats.
They talk of land, and day care, sales,
 closed deals, inheritance,
tax, secret affairs, and deadlines to
 meet, while she

detangles strings of thoughts, go back
 in time, rewrite the
walks on the beach and the pavements
 of a college street,
and the telephone booth that glistened
 in a corner of a dark,
empty curb where her jeepney ride
 used to stop.

NOEME GRACE C. TABOR-FARJANI

They took out the box years ago
    with the remains
of their arguments and apologies,
    and her calls for help.
The money she slipped into the coin
    slot would have been enough
for a ride home.
But she'd spend more for excuses
    to see him.
And he'd always come running,
    or driving to see her.
Please pick me up, or *drive me home, please.*

She looks to the shadows of arms expressing
    a story, while a coffee cup
cusped by hands, drinks the other's face,
    eyes, lips, smile, dreams.
Perhaps she tells, he pictures,
she writes and he films.
Like we used to do.

The window with its alternating shows of people
    and emptiness, busy, then languid,

REPRISE FROM SONG OF STARS

slowly twists and turns memory to hope
    and vice versa.
She waits for him, her back leans against
    the wallpaper, against time
and taboos, against tricks
her mind plays: *we cannot. ever be again. or*
    are we, have been.

Her pen taps on the oak, or is this mahogany?
    The light blinks for her take-out order,
just in case nothing happens on the pages
    she'll take a walk and carry
around her 16 ounce-cup to down 19
    years with it,
written on the recyclable plastic is
    Wonder Woman she
had whispered to the waiter, a joke
    she stole from him.
Recycled, like aged fallen stars,
    into that tiny meteorite
sheltered in a paper weight bell jar.

WHY I WRITE

If there is a reason for salvation, other than mercy, maybe it's self-love, or preservation. And perhaps, for courage and brilliance to surface as I spill onto the world what needs to come out from me, all those young girls, and ladies, and women. They, from the Book of Ruins: *crawl out of holes in pockets, and ripped hems, and buttonholes, alone. They hang on to strands of hair, dangling off a bun. Peep through cracked teeth. They are blisters from burned hands, popping out. Regrets that hide beneath folds of wrinkles, concealed by a smile.* I set them free. I have the keys, although sometimes I forget where I leave them, sometimes in kitchen works and domestic duties, and in the mazes of motherhood and *under so many rugs that hide the other women pulling me from wife. They prefer muse, the show, the stage, the salutations, their own name for wise. I hold them all together, sometimes in the cradle of forgetting which only their weeping and whining can bring me to remember.* That is what makes me brave and strong. I return to face and redeem what many chose to forget and leave behind. I reveal my shadows, but give them new colors and names that illumine with beauty so other women, those outside of me, friends, mothers, sisters, wives, tribe mates can battle shame of their darkness. From the place of utter weakness, a sufficiency of strength, the *me too*'s, and *I am you*'s. We are all the same, captives of a self, seeking a key that lies hidden inside. Only, not everyone knows that yet.

THE INBOX BECOMES
A CONFESSIONAL

What potential transgression does this to me?
I want to live holy, cling tightly
to common sense.

I try to endure this clawing from within
that wants to rip my little dignities open
just to see your eyes, smile,
and face again.

I clasp on to my pretensions
like patches for holes
you might notice—
controlled breathing, dry mouth,
uneven ways, not sure which hand
should pick the pistachios from your palm:

left, *no wait, let me put my phone down,*
hands seesaw: right, left, laugh
at the jitters you must have noticed

THE INBOX BECOMES A CONFESSIONAL

but I make excuses like an expert
for my *disorientation, brain fog.*

But it's not fog. It is smoke leaking
from the embers of middle age hormones
the whore moans
through a current of shame,

you probably suspect this is shyness
but I burn with wonder
dammit, is it just me, or you too?
and resistance
please don't look, don't come near.

I snuck my desires with my hand
under my pillow and insist
on that constant look of chagrin:
You hate me, no. Disgusted, maybe
or annoyed at my disheveled morality.
I hate me, too,

but I work hard on myself, make up
reasons to hate you. But those eyes
and face and smile. And
the pistachios in your palm.

WHIRLWIND IN MY MIND

This used to be a short-lived thought:
> *She sat on the couch last night,*
> *wondering through hastened breath*
> *if you on the other side also feel*
> *the sweet stirrings of residues*
> *from quick glances, and your name*
> *mentioned curtly instead of a hello.*
> *Did you wish to stay longer, too?*
> *Stare longer, even if it's only at her feet?*
> *Can one intentionally snap back*
> *awake while in rapid eye movement?*

Let me linger on this a little longer:
> *The coffee cup warms her hands*
> *as she leans against the door*
> *dividing your respective realities*
> *yet your face she sips from her cup,*
> *under the vast emptiness of sky*

WHIRLWIND IN MY MIND

*before her- grey buildings, grey pigeons,
grey glass windows, graying clouds
as colored movie scenes vibrate from
her chest no one will ever see.*

Unrequited love is a saleable narrative.
Wouldn't it be nice to be surprised
by fancies that come and ask to stay?
For exhilarating parts of youth to sneak
from behind the tail of our years,
like tiny fireworks that burst from
what we thought to be embers
of a dying romance?

SELF-REGULATION

this disaster of normalcy,
ill-starred by something close
to limerence, or lemon drops
and gumdrops. Is that even fine
for you to endure those eyes,
        and ears, mouth, nose,
        legs, hands, arms, chest,
        head and shoulders…
a nursery rhyme you hum
as a love song but like a child
doing homework, you create this
patchwork of uncharted territory
similar to kindergarten list of rules
directing you to: sit straight
        and still, eyes on the board, keep
        your hands to yourself, hold up
        those tears, suck in that breath,
        don't move, feet together…
tear
        your paper heart
                    apart.

ARS POETICA WITH DIALOGUES

I can economize, too, you know.
I can forgo verbosity and renounce
the lines lavished on blank sheet,
the lies of passion enmeshed
in a crumpled, satin blanket.
I can cut to the chase
and cut without bleeding
and stab the page straight
with a single-edged sword
with words like: *nothing* or *fine.*

I can write a twenty-six-year odyssey with you
in recurrent dreams, stalking and demonizing
my muse, profuse in metaphors I can abandon
as I get to the point, pointing at that cold ring
on a warm, empty passenger seat. *There goes*

bumping into you. *Thank you*, those
were kind words. You knew I'd make it.

NOEME GRACE C. TABOR-FARJANI

Water under the bridge, you say. *Right.*
And that ring, I tossed and lost
literally *under the bridge* too
strayed with infidelities and imitations
of making-up and making-out
they would have passed for a screenplay.

I can cut to the chase like you cut a scene,
and sin to your delight, deleting me but
I can economize too, all I've spent for you
in three words and my once cent:
It was nothing. Really.

I agree. *Bygones are bygones*,
like a multiple of *last time* we had. *Retakes*, you'd say.
I could be less wordy didn't I say? Small talk
doesn't cut to the chase. *Ok. Bye. See you around.*

I run to the ladies' room holding my chest like
a full porcelain piggy-bank ready to break
a thousand lines I've saved up for this day
my years of rehearsing, finally applauded
by a toilet bowl flushing,
my one minute of tears.

FOR ALTON,

ON THE PASSING OF THEIR GRANDMOTHER

As if loss is the unforgiving wind, soaking the remaining embers of what once was a bonfire until it turns to lingering smoke and ash, you wrote. But your vigil was not for the dead. It was for death itself to arrive. In rare musings, many hoped that it won't come like an explosion to run away from. A sudden death is merciless, leaving no light to return to, not even tiny flickers of warmth to soothe one's grief. There'd be wishes for loss to come ever so gently, like this. There is no sting to stories told but an almost eternal wake of memories we cannot bury, remain. A thousand hands cling on to us while we slowly loosen our grip on hope until we find ourselves unclasping them, one by one, day by day. We brush them woes off our sleeves, but they run back, tug at our hem, our heart, or sneak up on us, creeping into our dreams. Grief never really disappears. It just takes another form, like hope melding into concrete plans, vigils into visitations.

NOT A SEASON OF WRITING

Books and papers lay scattered
some notebooks on a tall pile.
Pens, here and there, black and blue.
I listen to my own tapping, summoning
Guidance or some user-manual, for *blah*
or bland days, to fall on my lap.
I attempt to pick on lines, browsing,
flipping pages, hoping to find
the elusive spark, a firefly of time.
I am charmed by the blank slate,
enchanted to stay, sit, dwell among
the ruins that hide underneath
the clean, smooth page.
It whispers to me to forget
the lines I wish to loan,
pass over the loots,
and do nothing.

ESCAPE ARTIST

I've said these before:
there are remnants of me in your works,
just as you are in my words. There is
no ritual for the sand we have become
in order to leave no trace of artifacts
of a muse we once shared. Some fossils
just do not sieve through forgetting.
And though we tried to disguise
our *infidelities with time*, we remained
heathens, drawn to each other's idols.
Did we not worship the movement of stars?

The pillage I hoarded from our ruins
proved to be useful in seasons of conjunctions.
When you referred to history, I have proof
of how you disappeared. And why.
But there is no point for a showdown
between hostages of the rivalry of gods.
You still scavenge for disguises, though.

ESCAPE ARTIST

You still feed on your tools for illusions
While vestiges of golden days crowd
under my feet, refusing to leave,
including scraps of memories
like cactus spines in my skin,
invasions I cannot escape.

THERAPY SESSION

How did this silence begin?
The withdrawal. I will
no longer play healer
to a root cause of pain.
Comfort Woman, how long
will you keep soothing
a predator's wound
your grandmothers once
drizzled with salted spit
straight out of their mouths
pouring like shakers of revenge,
their bellies acid-sour, revolt
fizzing up their throat.
Now you cradle their demon,
weeping on your lap
in a likeness that once ravished
the fullness of your ancestors' breasts.
His sorrow is for his arms
that missed a prey.
You kiss his cut, he sighs then gasps,

THERAPY SESSION

catching his breath while stealing
a glimpse of your glimmer.
His sly hands crawls to your chest
and grazes your heart, claws
at your fantasies. He digs
deep enough that you mistake
slow with gentle. He moans
in lustful agony that you mistake
strong with deep
like a dyslexion of feelings.
How long will this last?
'til you see the bleeding's
yours not his.

SURVIVAL TACTIC

I am trying to evade the hooks but desiring the
 baits
as I lurk a little beneath the surface like a
 potential catch
waiting for feeds that will sweetly disrupt the
 stillness of these waters.

I welcome a spillage of secrets and stories that
 shimmer through
the bubbles and all that seems to look good in
 forms of happy news,
presents, endearments, a wink, or kisses blown,
 a touch, or a lingerie,
candles, bath bomb, and the like, a little close
 to love.

I have mastered how this always goes: pretend to
 not know anything, but
give and give, laugh and dance, serve, smile and
 sing as if earth is water
and you're not gasping for air.

LEAVING

I'd have become a pillar of salt while leaving
    the check-in area
clutching our boarding passes, and looking
    back at everyone
I left behind.

It would have happened at the immigration row
    where I stood
sobbing and sniffling desires and despair as I
    clasped onto
my hand-carry.

My luggage filled up to its weight limit, kept my
    expired IDs,
migraine pills, and a journal of fantasies that
    tricked me
into a new faith.

I assumed that remembering means regretting,
    attachment is affection

while sentimental folly sugar coated my tears
    for home as well as
debts I have obtained.

I'd have been stricken with fire, if not for the
    tugging of grace- in faces
of my children who haven't been in an airport
    for years, I needed
to quicken my pace.

My husband told us to hurry, so I followed the
    airport crew led us on
as we evaded some brimstones of hate-speech
    that made me brave
but not bold enough to stay.

The moist heat in the lounge was but fever of
    lost homes that would have
hardened me like a monument of melancholy,
    and with this nostalgia,
a pillar of burnt sugar.

FOR NOW THERE
IS ONLY (IV)

For now there is only
this second coffee cup,
defying prohibitions:
should not
must stop
do decaf.

Moka pot brewed
with a dash of milk.
They say, *nothing beats Arabic*,
but this cup of artisanal arabica
tastes almost like my first drink:
instant, with cream
brand of the West,
produced in the East.

A thick residue of black pleasure
lingers after the last gulp.

NOEME GRACE C. TABOR-FARJANI

An imitated texture
of Mediterranean sand
settles under the silky liquid
topped with a semblance
of sweet fluffy clouds.
Still, the aftertaste of
the cheap yet well-blended
instant coffee remains
in my mouth.
This second cup
leaves me no after-effects
of sleeplessness
only a remembrance of its
residue of roughness.

PANIC ATTACK

I am uncertain if it is the ghibli   outside   threatening
to break the windows   or   the loud footsteps running,

running up and down   the stairs, or   back and forth
the door   that keep me   awake,   my eyes dilated
in this opportune time for sleep. But here it is, here is
a strong violation of peace at one am, not morning yet

yet doubt   throbs   in   my head   syncopating
with promises and pretensions crashing in my memory
like   family members   taking turns   in pumping
a manual   resuscitator bag   to sustain   their dying,

like hope albeit shredded at the seams of this familiar
long,   dark   night   haunting, returning.   I
should   have never   returned to where regrets
arrive way to early,   earlier   than the welcome

of one who left ghosts like orphans or orphans like ghosts banging, banging at the doorstep. Or wait, are they footsteps, racing? running,

running   up and down.

DISSIPATED RAGE ON VALENTINE'S DAY

How timely of you to ask if I ate the sugar block you left in the fridge.

It's in a cup, with a little water in it, you said.

Why would I do that? And yesterday would have been a better time to ask me that.

Or you could have at least put this off for tomorrow, this intrusion of my peace with guilt-trip.

Now I am about to lash out my defenses at you, for your many days of toil to ease me up, *let me write, leave me alone, give me back my silence*.

And oh, the children and the meals you make for them, the drive to school, sometimes the commute with a few pesos in your pocket enough for fare.

Who needs a wallet? Back and forth our chores, we ride on hope, sometimes we drive, sometimes we're driven maybe by love or fear of losing.

Now you want to pick on me. Your tongue probes through a possible lie or truth. *Sugar, sugar. Did you eat the sugar? Hmmmm...*

You straighten your back, leaving my mouth agape and a book I was about to slam on the table is suspended in my hand.

No, you did not, you smile while you savor the aftertaste of my mouth.

I throw my legs up and laugh. *Did you just...?* It's my turn to ask.

MY SON TELLS ME

Volcano eruption every 650,000 years,
my seven-year-old son, Zaki, tells me.
Maybe the world resets and begins with two people,
he says. *Maybe the world destroys itself
so life can happen again,* he tells me.

TEA TIME

I'm beginning to like empty words
like a cup half-filled with air bubbles
resembling soap suds.
Once I washed tiny tea cups
that were about to be served,
to my sister-in-law's dismay.
The froth I mistook for leftovers
spores from the drink.

They showed me how it's done and
served and sipped over small talk
like shots of joy that swiftly vanish.
But it is so good that I keep coming back
for more fix of half-truth, half froth
in the same old place, anywhere
on the floor.

They say the best one is here, kept
tradition, followed the old ways
though there are other types and colors
and ways to serve it, and cups to use.

TEA TIME

Of course, it is best when they never
stop pouring, be it green, or red, or black
or white. The bubblier, the better.

I stay through the fixes and simply agree
it is best when things don't change.
Every time. At everything said.
Bubbles don't hurt.

ADRIFT

Sometimes I'd lay
    in this twilight of a place
        and feel like I've never left,

like the home I returned to
    was just a figment of some deep sleep,
        a never-ending dawn.

And sometimes, it is a distant harbor
    where I look to my sail
        that perpetually waves for an anchor

aching to pull me back ashore,
    back to her, him, back to them all.
        This longing persists

between worlds, and joy
    pushing itself through dusk
        like the sea enduring the night.

SELF-SOOTHING

I wake up at four, clenching my dreams
    of home and other things
that remain unpacked, an entourage
    of orphans in the hallway
to my old room, waiting for my return
    to collect them back.
How can they fit here among belongings
    that never belong?
And longings that overstayed, turning into
    a favorite joke.

  I am consoled by an ability to *bear* and *endure*,
    and my propensity
  for these ever-handy euphemisms I have
    collected together with *regret*.
They resemble my corns and calluses that
    serve as skin padding
and protection for days like these,
    and many other

calamities of nostalgia, and hauntings
    at four am via dreams,
calling every old despair and doubt,
    a sacred destiny.

I pull up my blanket to caress the lavish cotton
    against my face.
I pull it higher, over my head, like a cozy,
    loving shelter of a home
I imagine going back to, celebrating the feast
    of pillows and comforter
as I continue painting them, daydreams on this
    canvass of a black night.

SEEING SHADOWS

I feel them returning, like a relapse
but not on bathroom tiles.

They must have followed me all the way here,
lodged themselves in pockets
of a mental luggage, these figures and shadows.

The stick drawings startle me, unaware
that they have been lurking, then creeping,
then suddenly disappearing, and sometimes
just swiftly passing, almost flashing on walls.

I feel them eavesdropping, sneaking, alerting me,
and yet they quickly hide, evading suspicions.

These bandits of joy, if not of despair, they scatter
fear camouflaged in the lining of blankets,
like a velvet sea covered with glitters.

FROM MEDITATION

I seek out meaning for this:
that I not move
an ancient boundary stone
set by my ancestors.

ancient landmarks
that have taken
the forms of parables,
and proverbs,
promises too,
I follow a path
set in stone,
they call a rock
that is higher.

JUNE IN REVIEW

I thought it is only 4. I was waiting, waiting,
for you to meet me here in my melancholy
until waiting turns to coping, watching Stutz,
trying to nap, and interrupting my escape
to take a video of myself talking
of counting the days, a line you twisted
as my hatred for this place.
Then you said we could leave.
That was my way out, an opening
where I said, *I'll see*.

It is strawberry moon. Our second full moon
tonight, ripe but I am waning, waning.
Perhaps the years have been too bright,
flashing an incurable light that strikes you
into denial of having me, always. Or maybe
you hate losing in a game I am not playing.
My hands are tired, beginning to hurt
From perpetually holding up the light.

for you. But I am still waiting, waiting.
That is my way in, an opening
where I could burn, as if the light
isn't enough for you.

TAILS OF THE LAST YEAR, IN WORDS

grief never really leaves us; it claims a permanent lodging while professing transience in luggage of memory; at times it opens the door, but only to welcome consolations, visiting; oftentimes, it sits by the window…

yet now it waits
   for freedom
      to bring along
         empty suitcases
            for my loot
               from wake after wake.
                  Consolations
                     from containers
                        of hand-me-down regrets,
                           worn once and then given away
                             as recycled frustrations
                               made of comic acts

    and choreography
    of happiness
  and defense
  mechanisms-
   sour, sweet, and
   into delicious denials
   that indulge our despairs.
   Relief goods shield us
    from the cold as we bundle up
    with them and then
   we wonder
   how in the world
   did we acquire
  an inheritance of heaviness.

I KNOW THIS FEELING, BUT

that devious elf creeps up again as I get on my
   knees to pray,
but merely clasping my hands and bowing my
   head my body curled,
supine, fetus-like in bed, brings no relief, no
   reins to clutch and stop
the thumping in my chest.

I mouth a faith that feels like straws in my
   tongue, tasting like bile
although I hope it was gold given the promises
   I was told.

I spin through the torment, the needle is a thorn.
I pace back and forth, between kitchen and
   bathroom, vacillating
between affirmations and doubt.

What is this "Not a thyroid issue, not a heart
   problem"

that blood tests and diagnostics could not
   name?

I hint on Mama's words:
   "I've been there, and your grandma and my
   cousins, too."
As if it's a tourist spot, an exotic symptom of a
   destination unknown.

   "You have to label, you must label"
said a colleague, prompting a battalion of
   theories rushing to my throat
but stopped at the edge of my tongue. I almost
   lashed out if not for my
expertise on sufferance, thanks to that blockage
   between throat and tongue.

I smile through clenched jaw and bit the words
   "You know nothing"
like a bitter pill I so wanted to shove on
   another's mouth.

I KNOW THIS FEELING, BUT

Sam reminds me of a Saturn return, the planet
 of this pain, while
a hundred google tabs of medical websites and
 research are left forgotten.

I stop the frantic guesswork and press my ears
 against the cold wall,
a consulate for amnesiacs.

AN HONEST EXCHANGE

Defying the gravity of grief with rage
I said to A who then replied:
    "How very Aries moon"
of me to storm in an office to demand
for answers to
    "Who calls the shots?"

They push my guilt button
but a current placement may dissolve
dreams, career, social status…
thus strengthens my commitment
to silent despair
    "How very Alpha,"
said Sami once, then-twelve, explaining:
    "You can do a hundred things
    like an expert and you can
    do them all at one time,
    and you are really fast."

AN HONEST EXCHANGE

I can put anyone in their place,
    but not that, not here.
    Alphas do not bottle-up their feelings,
    so that doesn't make me one.
        "You can only do everything."
    Except speak up, thanks.

I promise to send them
some wine next week.
We'll drink together
to our birth charts.

WRITING IN AUTUMN

The Ghibli here does not sashay
like Amihan used to, nudging me
to sit and write, caressing
my skin with gentle whispers.
I defend myself from the
austere, almost tyrannical tempest
bidding me to work, clean-up,
work, clean-up as if it's a master
of light and not the culprit
of fogging my plans with sand.
The cold, arid wind blows
particles that settle between
the tiny pleats in my hands,
they begin to resemble my stories,
brittle and refusing to ease themselves
ever so gently, softly, smoothly,
clear sentences on the page.
I am extra vigilant in this
sneaky weather, rushing
to write before the sky sends

WRITING IN AUTUMN

its rain amidst the flame of
summer sun. Before
it drenches my papers. But
the wind insists to dominate
my blank pages, hallow
with air and sounds.
I might just have
to wait for spring.

RECOVERY

Three days of gloom and doom, dizzy spells,
dullness, the devil himself licking my wounds
turn my body into an altar of scourging.
Soon after the fever subsides, light enters
through my door, like a rock that moved
and the huge, heavy, dark, cold,
opaque wall crumbles.

My hand gropes for water, my knees tremble
on the way to the sun, and I breathe in its light.
My arms, outstretched are like torches
that burn the residues of blame they call signs,
symptoms, causes, prognosis, synthetic,
curated placebos for an "itis"
diagnosed by saying "say ahh, open wider"
to see the tonsils, and pronouncing *congestion*.
Of what? Where? How? Is it a blockage
of words in my throat or mucus in my sinuses?

RECOVERY

The earth is a hundred meters far below
my feet held by the cold, marble floor.
I press my hands on the soil of the balcony
planter, and drink the air, inhale through
my nose, exhale through my mouth.
Suddenly I am hungry for real food,
not soup, or lemon-ginger-turmeric-mint tea,
not saltine crackers but rice and meat.

Suddenly, my eyes no longer squint at light
anymore. Each sun ray, bird sound,
movement gently pulls out my
tender feelings towards pain,
the devil cannot delegate the
wound-licking to my alkaline,
non-acidic tongue.

CHECK UP

I expect to get some bloodwork done
and an explanation for the dry spells

and mental block, too.

She shrugs, looking stunned
that I speak her language.
I have more words for her dire need
of extra effort to follow her Hippocratic oath.
But I keep to myself and pretend to understand

that blood work is not a necessity
and Panadol infusion will do.

Post-nasal drip, fever, joint pains
due to severe sinus infection,
threatening an onset of tonsilitis.
I could have been a doctor of bodies
having read their four-consonant textbook
for diagnosis and treatment,

CHECK UP

side by side symptomatic healers
concocting words, oil and herbs like
my Shaman friends.

She tells me to take a three-day rest.
Somehow, I knew like kindred
of wounded healer hands,
in my private valley of skulls
I must lay my head down, and wait
for the rock to move.

RACING THOUGHTS

what poem or brilliant piece
can be written in a cage railed
with time? say, three minutes
to chase the rushing thoughts
that once beat my grief down,
I even forgot why I cried.
I hurry to catch
the decadent drippings of mind
as in a rendezvous in prison,
sweet, lucid yet brief,
a possibility that quickly
escaped me
like a winged creature
unfit for race or flight
but finding its home
along the finish line, finished
like tired runners, resembling
desires that eloped with guilt.
I brought myself upon this.

FROM THE JOURNAL OF EXISTENTIAL DREAD

The world is as it should be, needing
    no salvation. Contrast is a prescription
for survival, like despair for hope or breath
    for nothingness.

We may burn the pages we flip, like movable
    bridges that turn over, but get
them people moving- those who linger longer
    to drink more of the river view.

A bridge, too, is a view of passersby, harried,
    in a hurry, not sightseeing.
Travelers, and settlers of double lives shuttle
    the path, to and fro, reload, unload
cargos of memories, dismantle and rebuild
    from grief and hope.

NOEME GRACE C. TABOR-FARJANI

Farewells do not happen but only longer hellos
    on both ends. And sometimes,
longer promises are spoken in the eternal
    in-between almost impossible to reach
or return to.

We keep moving, and doing what needs be. We
    keep arriving at the same place
of longing and wonder- for what's left behind
    and for what is to come.

Movement is an ever-present dance of memory
    and hope, although sometimes,
regret cuts in, and doubt shuts the music down.

At times, the sound of a moving bridge deafens
    us to its warning, as it flips over
and we are overturned, poured over, to become
    the water under the bridge.

IN MY LIVING ROOM

The ghosts would like it here, those from days of old, of an orgy that is a devouring of delicious, rhythmic evenings. Gut. Wrenching. Highness.

Rolling Stones and Aretha take turns from the red and blue light flashing portable speakers, but there are no smoke rings like the ones in the old piano bar where I used to work. I. Speak. Easy. To. Bring. Me. Back to life.

They'd love this shelf in black and orange vinyl finish, and the fuchsia velvet robe draped on my chair, that would fog with their shameless drag if they were here. The. Way. They. Used to do in dimly lit lounges for the half-dead. Sweet purging of a revolt that refused the placards and shouting in the streets.

So. They. Do. It. There. Then. And here, playing jazz they'd call subtle and cool, with saxophone and trumpet and loud defiance of too-muchness. I ponder about what too much means to them as their bebops and voices in my music player fill this room.

Now remains their memory in my abstract cover-up, and pop-art heart on my sleeve, and grunge-smeared face, and hoop earrings, boho trinkets, and warm lights from the oil diffuser lamp and antique crystal glasses where their apparitions seem to merge. I delude them, alive.

Everything is thick and rich and heavy, strong. But they'd feel at home here, among the bronze plaques, and dark wooden guest table with cracked glass cover, gold and red couch, and turquoise and purple linens and mandala curtains.

Such rich materials to showcase their anti-materialism. But it's their revolt I am after.

IN MY LIVING ROOM

Of the unalive. And brave. And transient. Temporary revolutionaries, ghosts faked by my ancestors. What a haunting for protests undone.

They might have possessed me in my imitation of freedom in this dot of the Maghrub. And my moonlighting commences every time I step in, not out, of this room.

VISIONS

slow moving droplets from clouds   glitters
while   melted gold glide through a   transparent wire
with streaks of rain that's made of light.   smooth brass
of rails, cold, liquid crystal   pouring down my ears, throat,
gently tingle   in my chest. underneath are ruins made of
silver dust, once a rough rock bursting into shimmers of fire
the rays of spring   usher these   visions of   a night
laced with   stars that make me want to   burst   too.

BIRDHOUSES
IN BULLET HOLES

there is no time to make pigeon holes,
the wasteland walls will do
as dwelling for these remnants
salvaged among a thousand
last breaths

there is no need for peepholes
for we are under an open sky,
a far cry from our fortresses
that have crumbled.

no need to muffle our voices,
as our ears are now deaf,
thanks to shelling
and explosives
that numbed our hearing,
it's a wonder how they

assign those nouns
as adjectives to podiums
and lecture halls.

no need for ornaments,
our wings, and houses
in bullet holes are enough
to decorate a citadel
that stands proud
above the vast ruins.

AFTER THE SANDSTORM

Now it's quiet,
its voice loaned from the trees,
sand, and loosely hinged doors
has disappeared.
I clean up and spit out
the aftertaste of sand,
watch the bath water
turn to brown as it slithers
down my body and
to the drain.
I step out to witness
the resumption
of exuberant exchange
between sky and land
as if the storm was a passing joke,
and its proudest moment was to think
of itself as sand, not as the steady air
I breathe while cleaning the mess
it left behind.

SETTLEMENT

every time   I touch my heart,
it tells me   to be still,
like a religion   of knowing
without knowing how
or why   there is no path,
trigger,   or switch
of light   but eternal safety
underwater, an immunity
to storms   of the deep,
dark,   and quiet secure
from a life sentence
of straining the neck,
eyes,   and feet
constantly running,
looking   up,
chasing   the sky.

IN MY HOUSE BACK HOME

I am not cleaning the house.
Not just yet. Because she is there,
just there inside a house I left behind,
keeping on, moving on
along the same dotted
lines we trace our dreams
quietly, convinced
we chose the right thing
to stay. I here, she there
in the same light.

I gave birth to a dose
of my own medicine,
not quite bitter,
not quite sweet,
a bite I need to swallow
every single day
until it becomes a part
of me.

NOEME GRACE C. TABOR-FARJANI

I am regretfully the best of all
in the dark, where no one
can see, whom no one sees.

SWIM THEN FLY AWAY

and dive deep down, leave the shores
to their thorns, broken glasses camouflaged
in their crystalline sands. swim far, never
to be found again no matter how long
they lay, waiting in vigil for your songs

of an illness of anticipation,
malady of remembering
how it was and so it should be
when it should not really be this way
when there was no known cure
for a made-up disease
created out of memory

ask for a vision, not dreams anymore
I ask

> how to be lost without disappearing
> how to be lost but not disappear
>
> oh to be lost yet not disappear!
> oh to disappear but never perish!

REFLECTIONS ON POEMS AND ON RETURN

Returns are an ever constant yet impermanent theme in spaces I inhabit. The twigging thoughts, diversions, escape, retreat, and sometimes, sudden cowering of the mind from an assault of memories are pathways of returning.

Whether come back to where we are, go back to where we used to be, or to revisit old hopes or bury decaying guilt, these lucid intervals require to leave parts of us in order to reach places we have forgotten, including the people we once were. Returning means remembering, including the future we created once upon a time through the portals built from our roots. These ideas, "built from previous knowledge" they'd say, have beginnings in which we have no way of knowing, unless we return to our stories of things, ancestors, places, movements, bodies, and the intangibleness of raw emotions that occupied our human experience. Returning means re-viewing, either from a different perspective or from a renewed perception. It may

REFLECTIONS ON POEMS AND ON RETURN

be problematic to determine who is the returnee and where is the exact place of arrival, given the transient nature of homecoming. As soon as we arrive at a destination, the unpacking, sorting, and shelving become transports to memories, new and old. For a long time, we are wrapped in the safe comfort of mistaking returns with settlement. With the myriad daily vehicles of thoughts—in revenge, desire, forgiveness, resentment, guilt, hope—it is clear that none of us will ever be settled.

This is the best way for me to survive journeys after journeys, to and fro the other side of clarity and sanity.

Noeme Grace C. Tabor-Farjani, PhD
Summer 2024 (Tripoli, Libya)

www.ingramcontent.com/pod-product-compliance
Lightning Source LLC
Chambersburg PA
CBHW020542080526
44583CB00013B/960